Going to
Hospital
By
Joanna
Brundle
BookLife

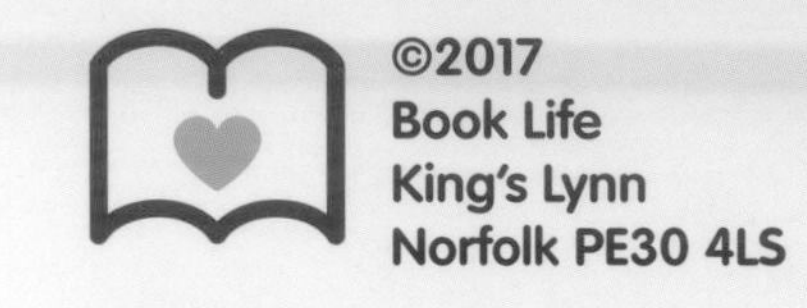

©2017
Book Life
King's Lynn
Norfolk PE30 4LS

ISBN: 978-1-78637-071-6

Printed in Malaysia

A catalogue record for this book is available from the British Library.

Written by:
Joanna Brundle

Edited by:
Grace Jones

Designed by:
Danielle Jones

Contents

What is a Hospital?

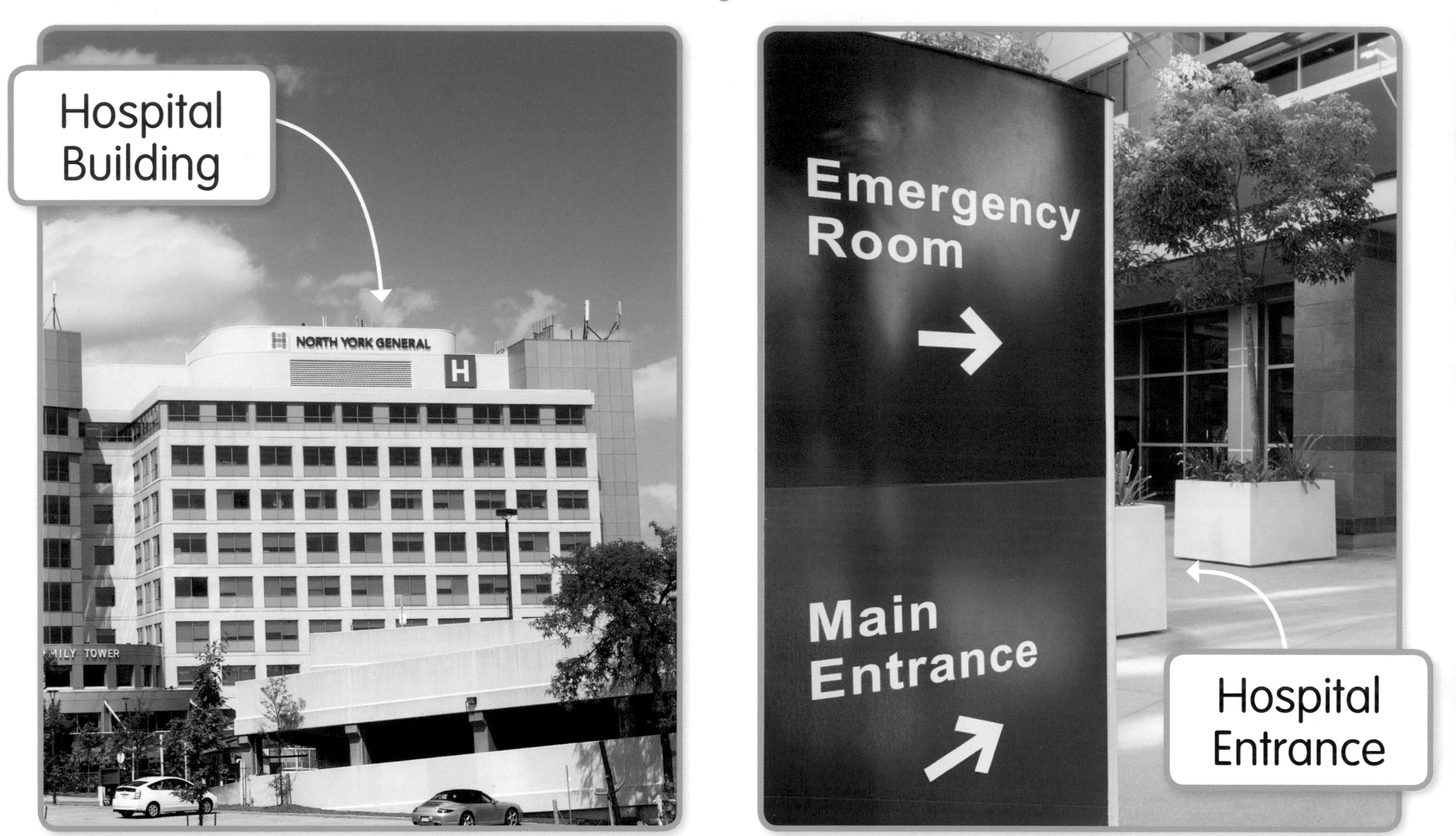
Hospital Building
NORTH YORK GENERAL
H
Emergency Room
Main Entrance
Hospital Entrance

A hospital is a place we go to when we are very poorly.

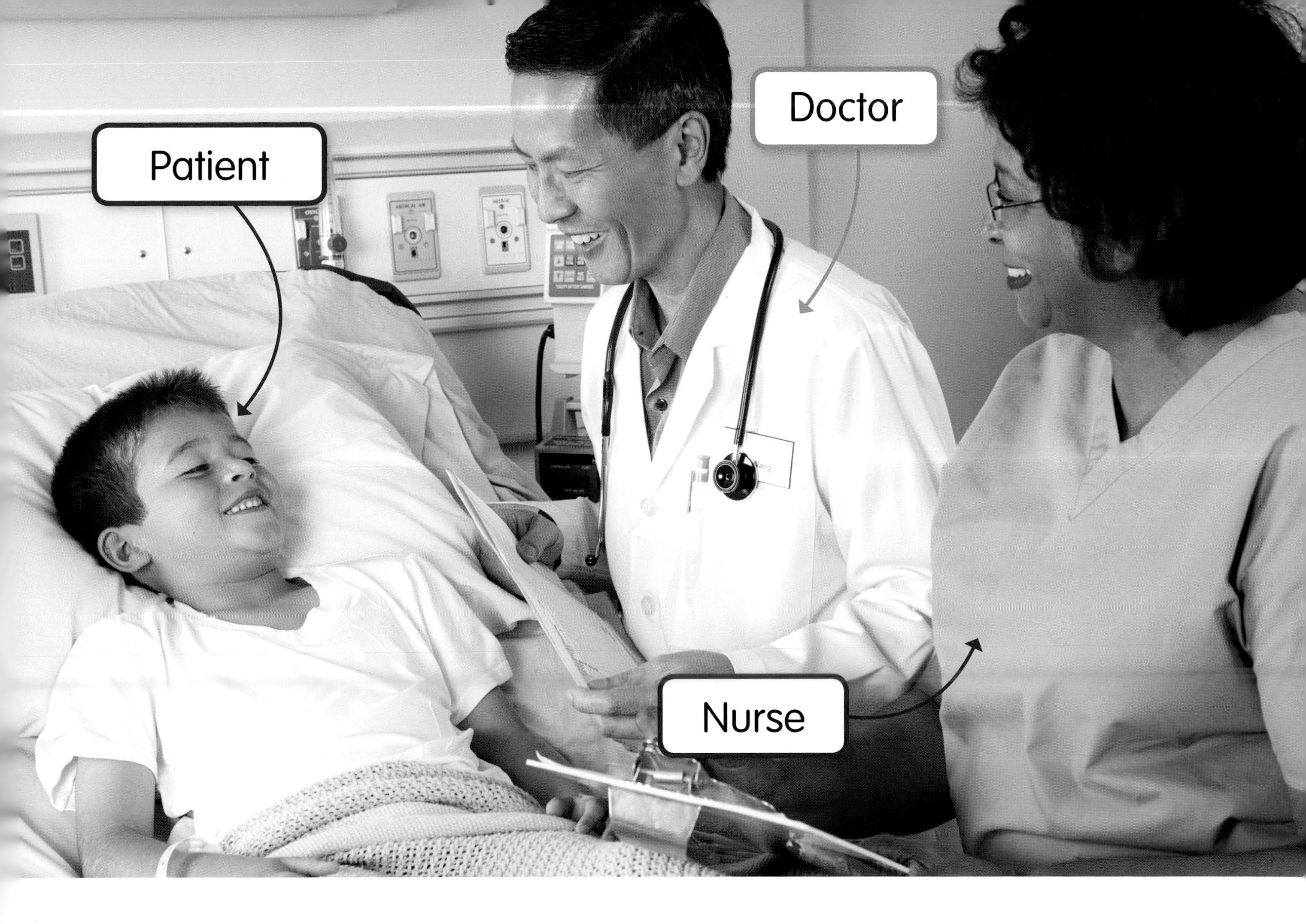
Patient
Doctor
Nurse

Hospitals are big, busy places that are full of patients, doctors and nurses.

Why do we go to Hospital?

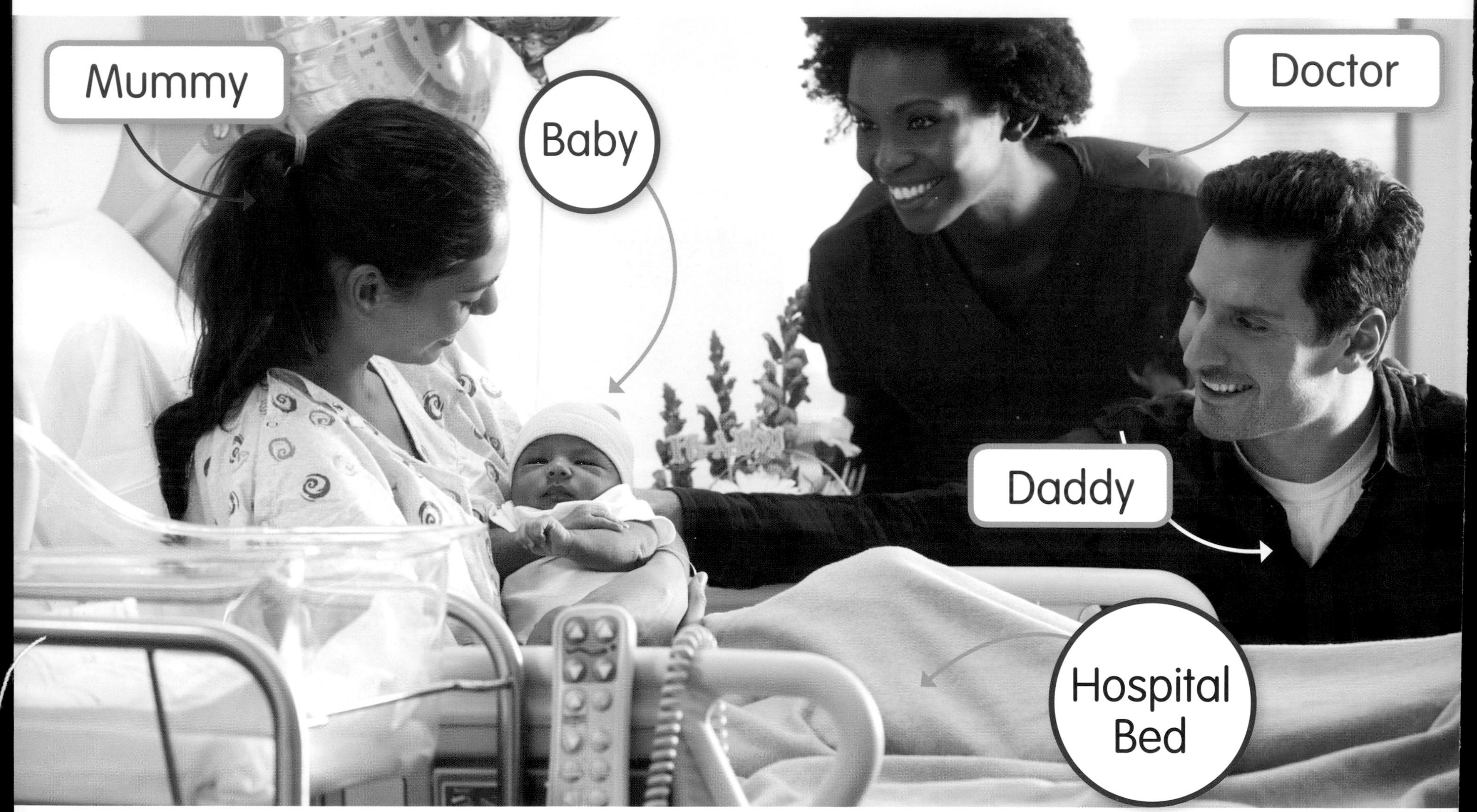
Mummy
Baby
Doctor
Daddy
Hospital
Bed

Most babies are born in a hospital. Were you?

We go to hospital if we have an accident.

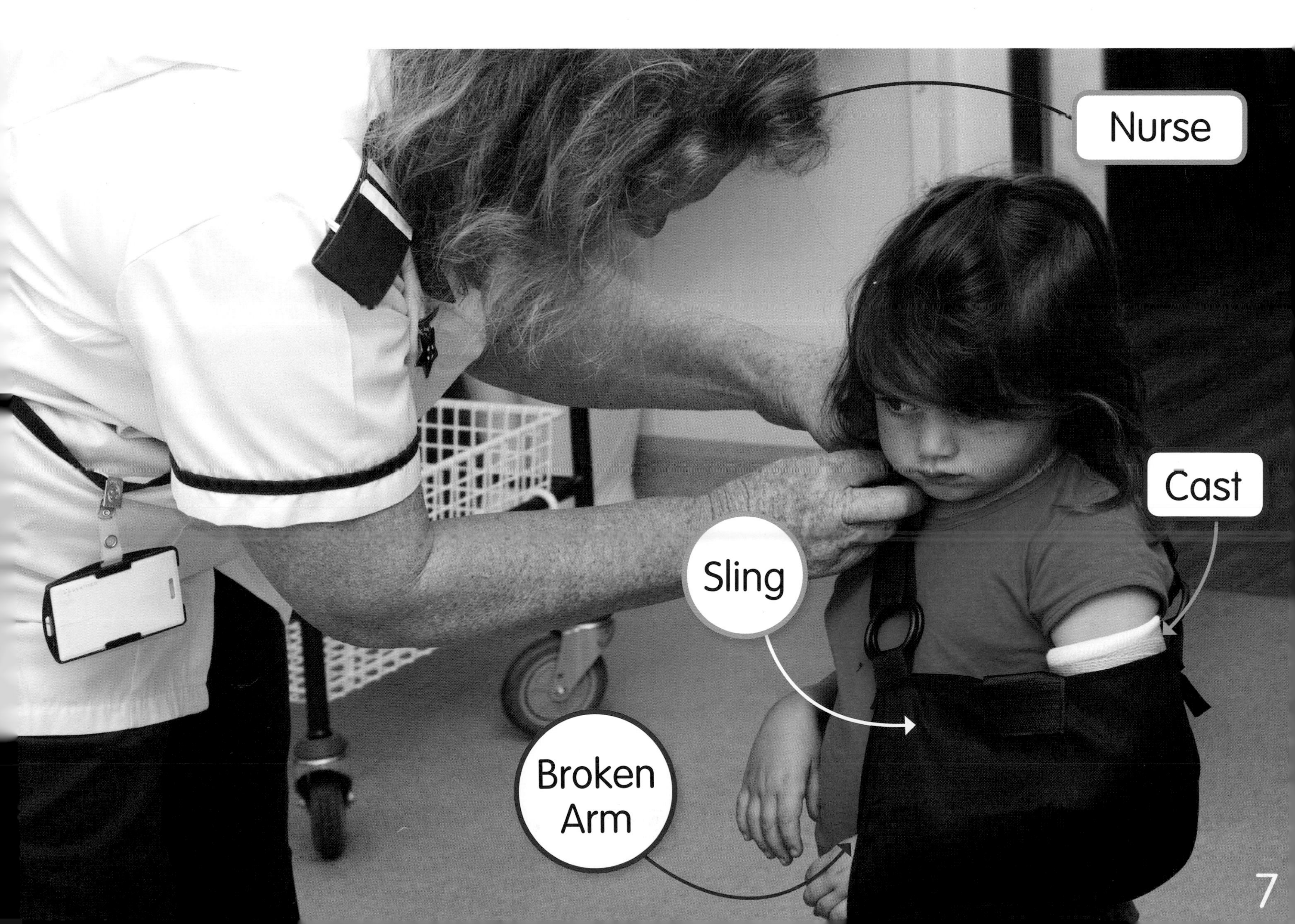
Nurse
Cast
Sling
Broken Arm

Checking
Throat
Checking Ears

Sometimes we need special tests or care.

X-rays and scans show us how our insides look.
They don't hurt.

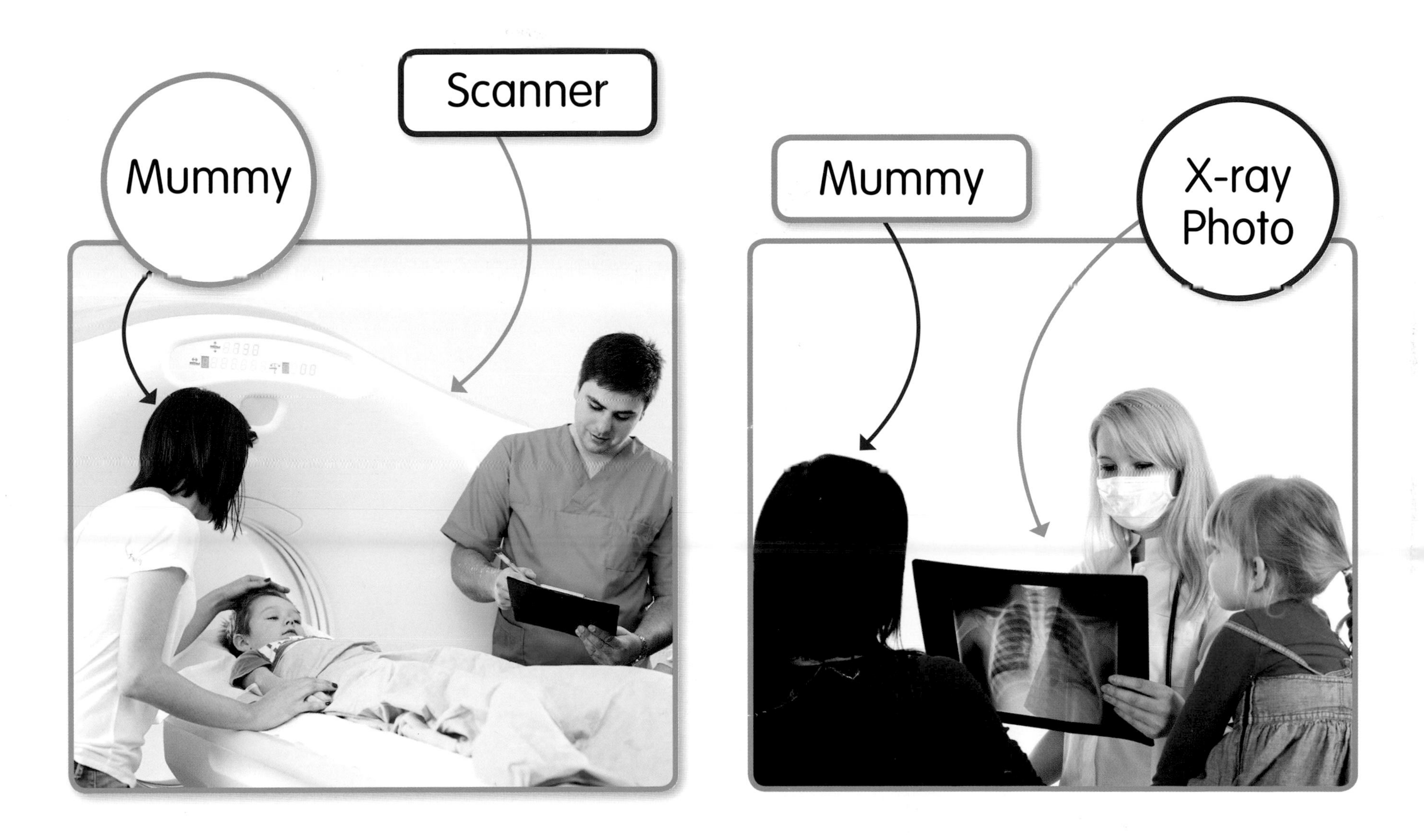
Mummy
Scanner
Mummy
X-ray
Photo

How do we go to Hospital?

We might go to hospital by car or in a wheelchair.

Teddy
Nurse
Bandage
Wheelchair

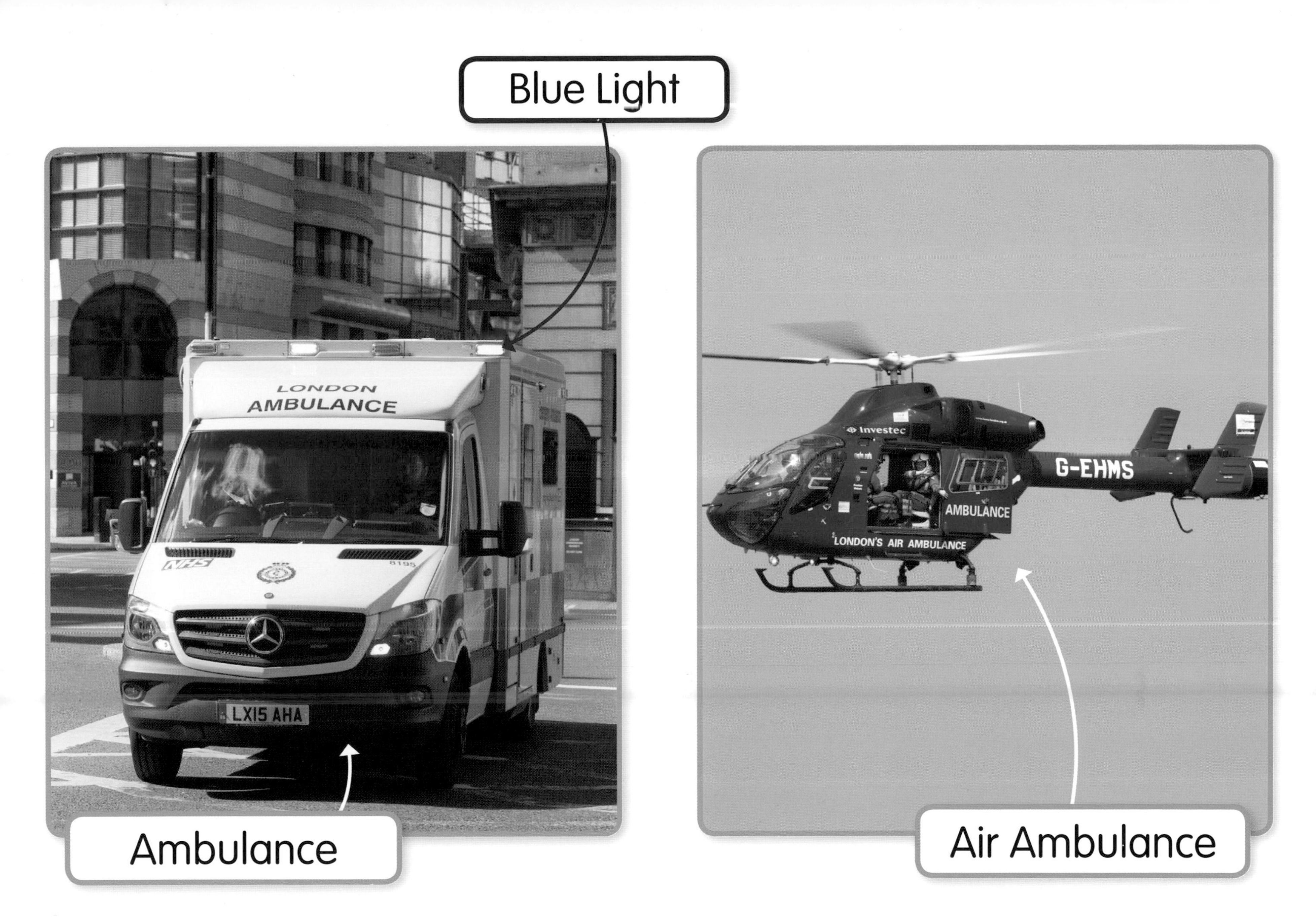
Blue Light
LONDON
AMBULANCE
LX15 AHA
Ambulance
Investec
G-EHMS
AMBULANCE
LONDON'S AIR AMBULANCE
Air Ambulance

If we are very poorly, we go in an ambulance or an air ambulance.

Who Looks After us in Hospital?

Doctor
Doctor's Uniform
Nurse
Nurse's Uniform

Doctors and nurses take care of us. They usually wear uniforms.

They sometimes wear gloves and masks to keep germs away from us.

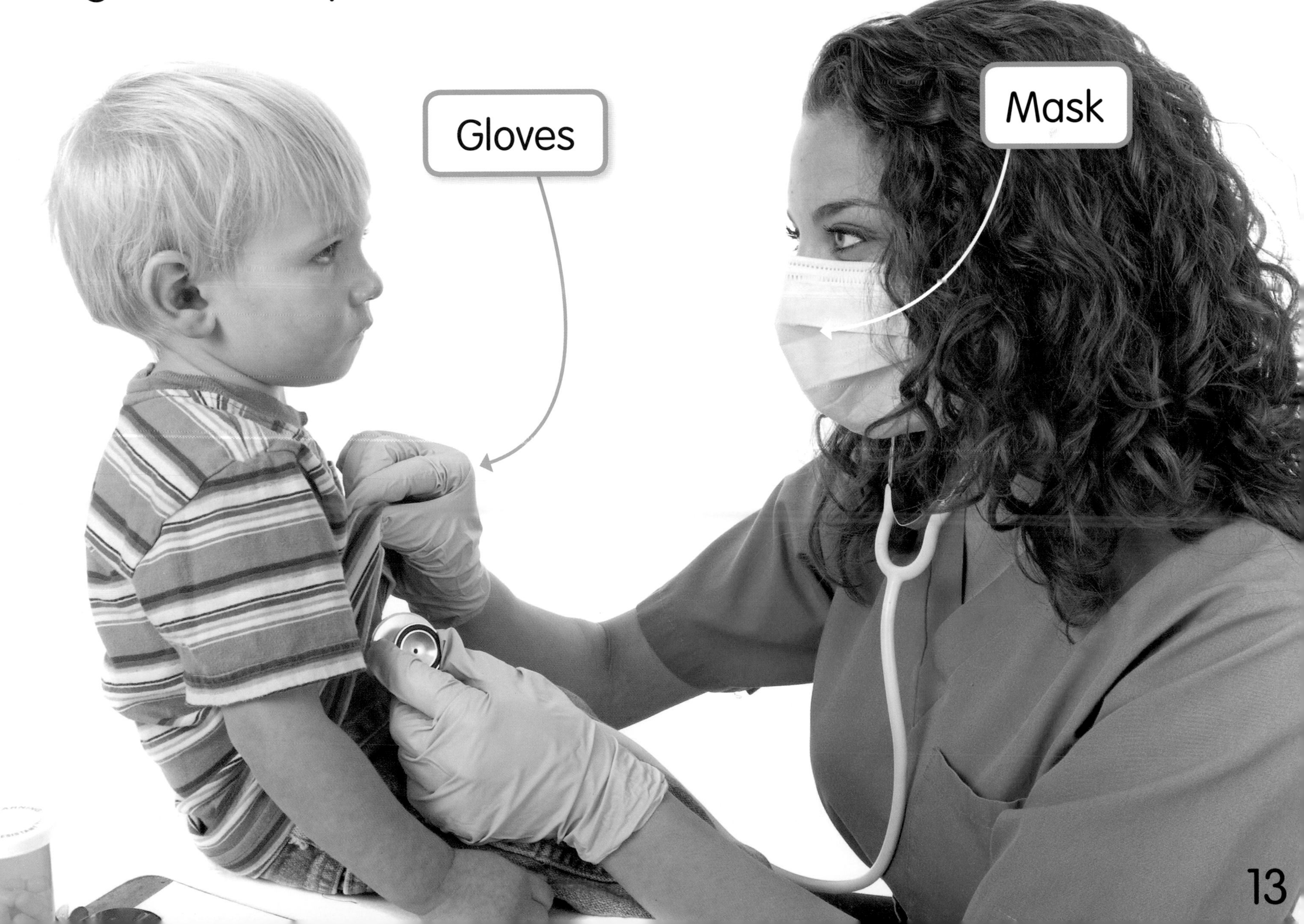
Gloves
Mask

The doctor decides the best way to look after us.

X-ray
Photo
Doctor

Say Aaah!

The nurse gives us our medicine and takes our temperature.

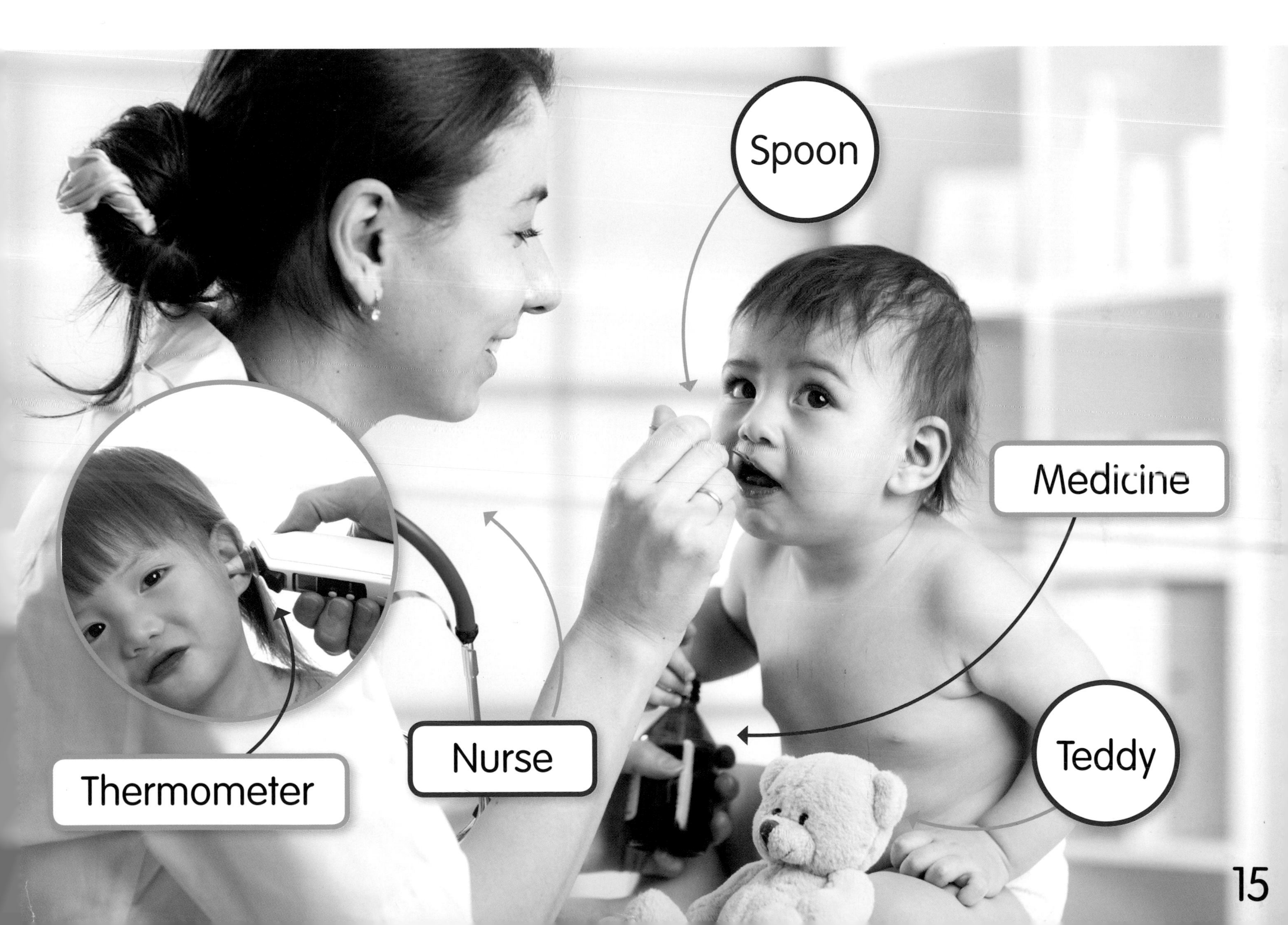
Spoon
Medicine
Nurse
Thermometer
Teddy

I Spy . . .
Stethoscope
Doctor

The doctor uses a stethoscope to listen to our chest or tummy.

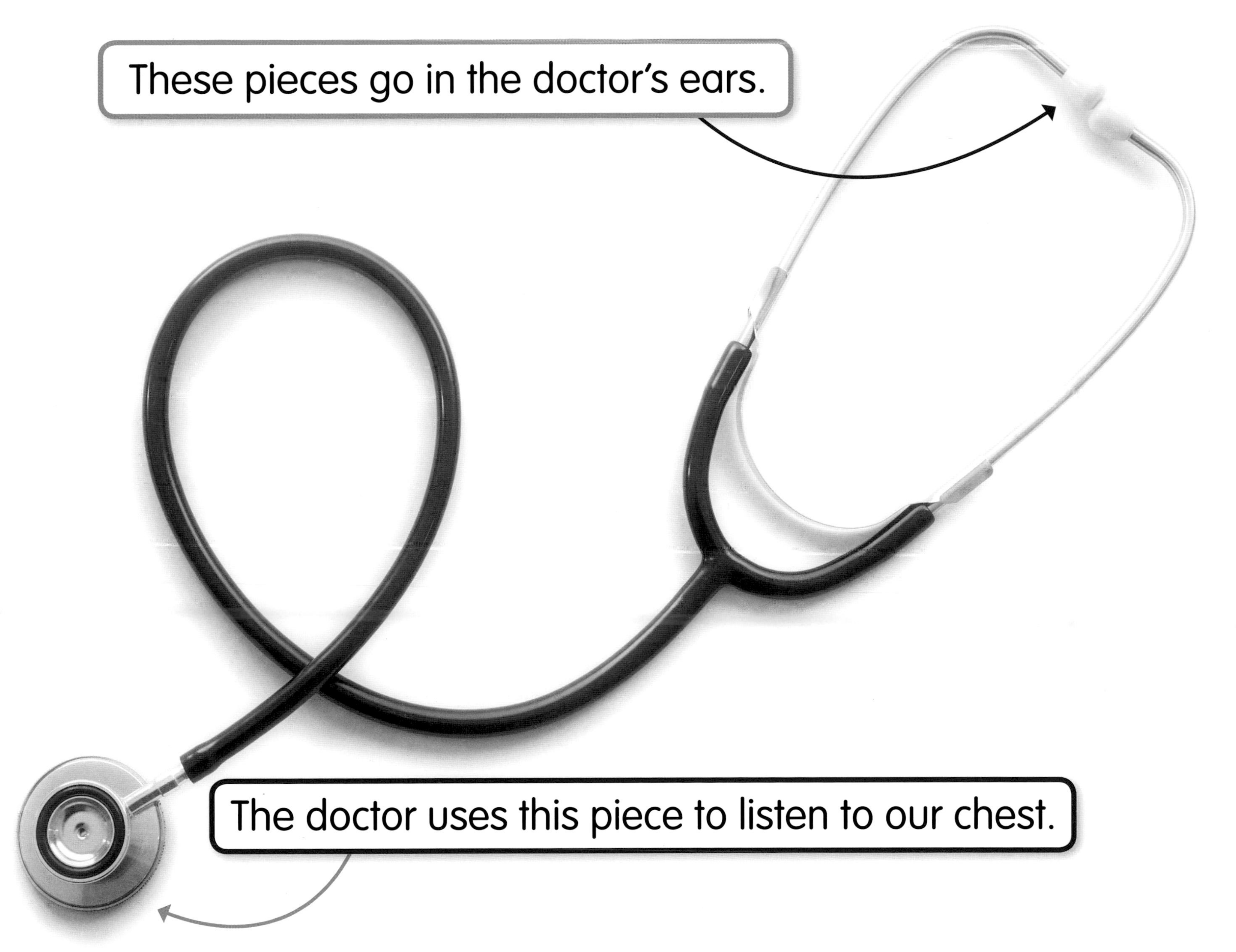
These pieces go in the doctor's ears.
The doctor uses this piece to listen to our chest.

Inside a Hospital

Waiting Room
Magazines
Chairs
Table

The waiting room is where we wait before we see the doctor.

The bedrooms are called wards. The beds are on wheels.

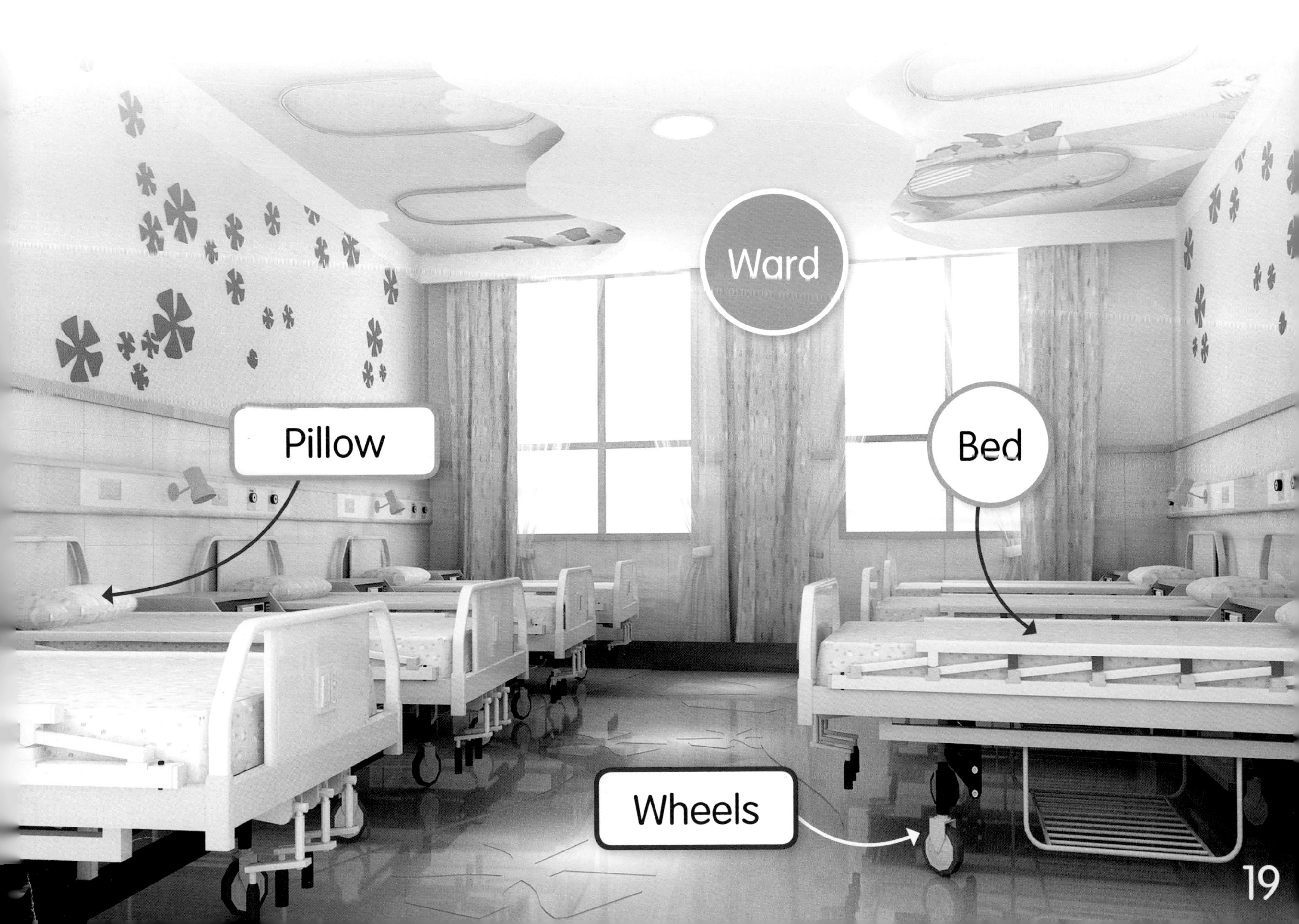
Ward
Pillow
Bed
Wheels

Staying in Hospital

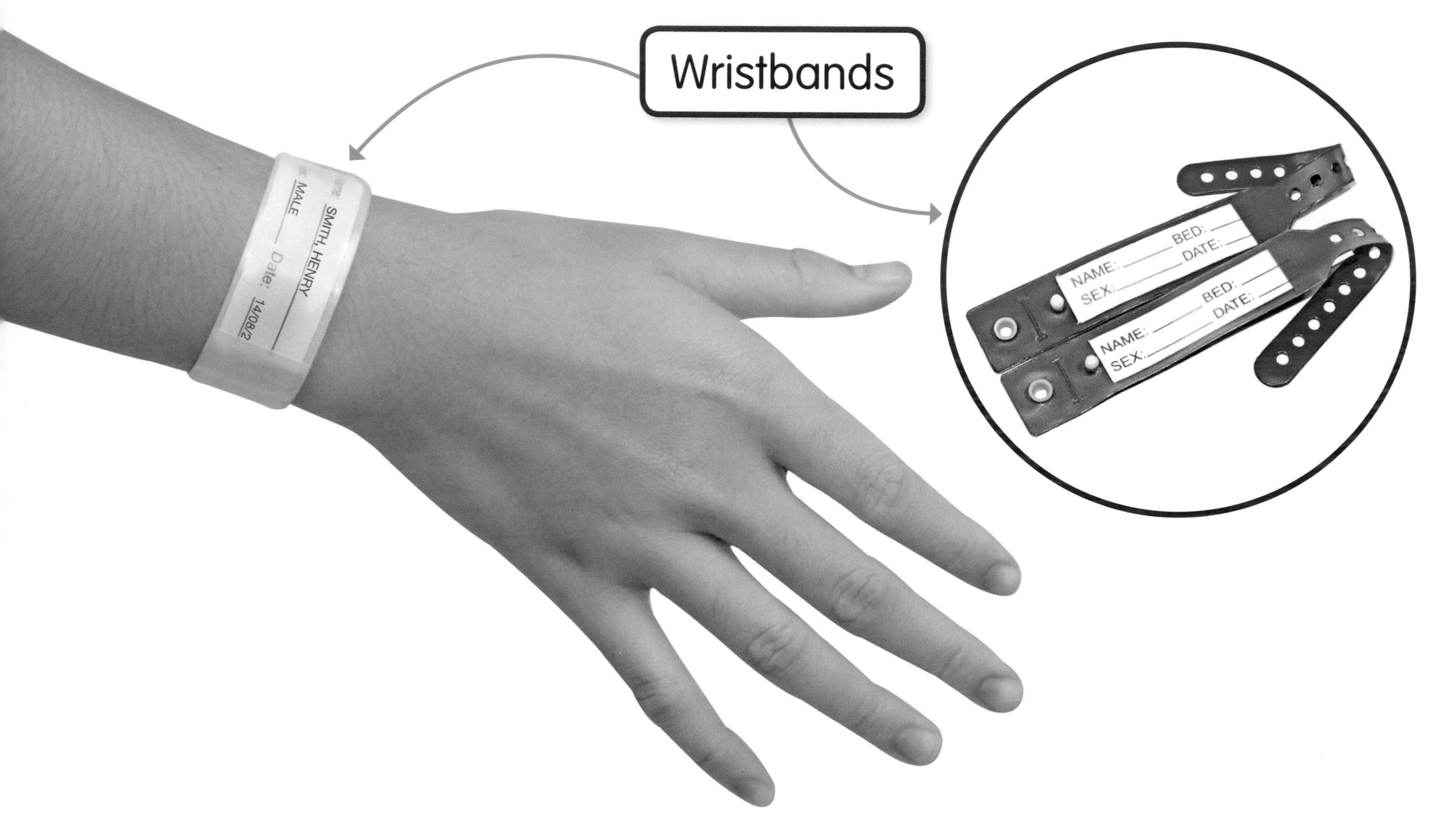
Wristbands
SMITH, HENRY
MALE
Date: 14/08/2
NAME:
SEX:
BED:
DATE:
NAME:
SEX:
BED:
DATE:

We wear a special wristband that tells the doctor who we are.

We wear a special gown and sometimes stay in bed for our meals.

Gown
Drink
Wristband
Apple
Fork

Leaving Hospital

Bed
Tablet
Medicine
Teddy

At home, we have to rest and keep taking our medicine.

We might have to go back to the hospital for a check-up.

High-five!
Fit and well!

Index

Photo Credits

Abbreviations: l-left, r-right, b-bottom, t-top, c-centre, m-middle.

Front Cover l – VGstockstudio Front Cover ml– Spotmatik Ltd Front Cover mr – wavebreakmedia Front Cover r – Oksana Kuzmina. 1 – Oksana Kuzmina. 2 – Pressmaster. 3 – Oksana Kuzmina 4l – mikecphoto 4r – Monkey Business Images. 5 – Monkey Business Images. 6 – Monkey Business Images. 7 – ChameleonsEye. 8l – wavebreakmedia 8r – goodluz. 9l – Olesia Bilkei 9r – photomak. 10 – michaeljung. 11l – IR Stone 11r – Paul Drabot. 12l – Andresr 12r – michaeljung. 13 – KellyBoreson. 14l – lenetstan 14r – AVAVA. 15 – Oksana Kuzmina 15 inset – Thomas M Perkins. 16 – michaeljung. 17 – Production Perig. 18 – avarand. 19 – wxin. 20 – Praisaeng 20 inset – Sto. 21 – wavebreakmedia. 22 – Tomsickova Tatyana 22 inset – Boris Ryaposov. 23 – gpointstudio. Images are courtesy of Shutterstock.com. With thanks to Getty Images, Thinkstock Photo and iStockphoto.